250
3in

D0094085

MEET MY FOLKS!

MEET
MY
FOLKS!

Ted Hughes

faber and faber

LONDON · BOSTON

First published in 1961
by Faber and Faber Limited
3 Queen Square London WC1N 3AU
Reprinted 1967, 1970
This revised edition first published as a Faber Paperback in 1987

Phototypeset by Wilmaset, Birkenhead, Wirral
Printed in Great Britain by
Redwood Burn Ltd, Trowbridge, Wiltshire
All rights reserved
Text copyright © Ted Hughes 1961, 1977, 1987
Illustrations copyright © George Adamson, 1961, 1977, 1987

British Library Cataloguing in Publication Data

Hughes, Ted
Meet my folks!—2nd ed.
I. Title   II. Adamson, George, 1913–
821'.914   PZ8.3

ISBN 0–571–13644–3

for
FRIEDA REBECCA

Contents

I've heard so much about other folks' folks,
How somebody's Uncle told such jokes
The cat split laughing and had to be stitched,
How somebody's Aunt got so bewitched
She fried the kettle and washed the water
And spanked a letter and posted her daughter.
Other folks' folks get so well known,
And nobody knows about my own.

12

My Sister Jane

And I say nothing – no, not a word
About our Jane. Haven't you heard?
She's a bird, a bird, a bird, a bird.
Oh it never would do to let folks know
My sister's nothing but a great big crow.

Each day (we daren't send her to school)
She pulls on stockings of thick blue wool
To make her pin crow legs look right,
Then fits a wig of curls on tight,
And dark spectacles – a huge pair
To cover her very crowy stare.
Oh it never would do to let folks know
My sister's nothing but a great big crow.

When visitors come she sits upright
(With her wings and her tail tucked out of sight).
They think her queer but extremely polite.
Then when the visitors have gone
She whips out her wings and with her wig on
Whirls through the house at the height of your head –
Duck, duck, or she'll knock you dead.
Oh it never would do to let folks know
My sister's nothing but a great big crow.

At meals whatever she sees she'll stab it –
Because she's a crow and that's a crow habit.
My mother says 'Jane! Your manners! Please!'
Then she'll sit quietly on the cheese,
Or play the piano nicely by dancing on the keys –
Oh it never would do to let folks know
My sister's nothing but a great big crow.

My Fairy Godmother

When I was born the Wicked Powers as usual were
waiting.
One said: 'This boy will build with bricks already
disintegrating.'
Another said: 'Sometimes his eye will be flat and
sometimes round.'
Another: 'Like a razor will come every little sound.'

Another said: 'The earth for him will have such magnet
strength
It will drag all things from his hold, and his own body at
length.'
Another said: 'For him, the golden beauties that he
grasps
Will turn one half to mist and one to biting poisonous
asps.'

Another said: 'A misty rock is all this boy shall be.
He shall meet nothing but ships in distress and the
wild, empty sea.'
Another: 'He shall be a ghost, and haunt the places of
earth,
And all the stars shall mark his death as little as his
birth.'

The Wicked Powers, the Wicked Powers, they crowded
  to have their say,
And all that day they said it, but at the end of day
My Fairy Godmother stood up, the one Power on my
  side:
Brighter than any dawning sun, whiter than any bride.

'You will need this,' she said to me, where I lay
  powerless.
Two sticks of sugar she gave me, lemon-flavoured if
  you please.
'These will save you everywhere, because because
  because
I stick them together and make them a ladder to lift you
  out of loss.
The ladder will change and change and change, just
  cling to it whatever –
It will twist and spiral, just you climb up it forever –

Climb this ladder, climb it, then the will of the Wicked
  Powers
Will dribble harmless off your heels, like the water of
  April showers.'
She said this and she gave me a thing too tiny for the
  eye
But with a smile I never shall forget until I die.

'Sail the wide sea,' she said, 'And cross the broad land,
But take this little ladder though you cannot
  understand.
And when your children come to the world, break off a
  piece for each.
It will grow whole for all of you, and lift you from the
  reach

Of waiting Wicked Powers, and their stupidity.
This very, very tiny thing, so far too tiny to see –
This is the magic gift by which you shall remember me.'

She vanished and the Wicked Powers vanished and I
grew,
And what I remember of that day I tell it here to you.

My Grandpa

The truth of the matter, the truth of the matter –
As one who supplies us with hats is a Hatter,
As one who is known for his growls is a Growler –
My grandpa traps owls, yes, my grandpa's an Owler.

Though owls, alas, are quite out of fashion,
Grandpa keeps busy about his profession
And hoards every owl that falls to his traps:
'Someday,' says he, 'they'll be needed, perhaps.'

'Owls are such sages,' he says, 'I surmise
Listening to owls could make the world wise.'
Nightlong his house is shaken with hoots,
And he wakes to owls in his socks and his boots.

Owls, owls, nothing but owls,
The most fantastical of fowls:
White owls from the Arctic, black owls from the Tropic.
Some are far-sighted, others myopic.

There are owls on his picture frames, owls on his chairs,
Owls in dozens ranked on his stairs.
Eyes, eyes, rows of their eyes.
Some are big as collie dogs, some are thumb-size.

Deep into Africa, high into Tibet
He travels with his rubber mouse and wiry owl-net:
The rarest of owls, and the very most suspicious
Will pounce on the mouse and be tangled in the
    meshes.

'Whatever you could wish to know, an owl will surely
    know it,'
My grandpa says proudly. 'And how does he show it?
Sleeping and thinking and sleeping and thinking –
Letting a horrible hoot out and winking!'

Grandma

My grandmother's a peaceful person, and she loves to
sit.
But there never was a grandma who was such a one to
knit.

Scarves, caps, suits, socks –
Her needles tick like fifty clocks
But not for you and not for me.
What makes her knit so busily?

All summer wasps toil tirelessly to earn their daily
dinner,
Their black and yellow jerseys getting shabbier and
thinner.

Grandma knows just how a wasp grows
Weary of its one suit of clothes.
She knits flowered skirts and speckled pants –
Now they can go to the beach or a dance.

Under the ice the goldfish hear December blizzards
beating.
They have no fire at all down there, no rooms with
central heating.

So when frost nips the lily roots
Grandma's knitting woolly suits –
Greens, blues, the goldfish adore them!
Winter-long they're thankful for them.

When snowy winds are slicing in through all the little
   crannies
The shrubs and birds in our neighbours' gardens envy
   those in my granny's.

Her shrubs have scarves and pullovers,
Her birds have ear-muffs over their ears,
And cats that come asking for 'Titbits please'
Go trotting away with little bootees.

A frosty Octopus received a stout eight-fingered mitten.
A Camel whose important hump tended to get
   frost-bitten

Has a tea-cosy with tassels on it.
A grass-snake has a sock with a bonnet.
Folks can buy clothes at some shop or other.
The creatures depend on my grandmother.

My Other Granny

My Granny is an Octopus
   At the bottom of the sea,
And when she comes to supper
   She brings her family.

She chooses a wild wet windy night
   When the world rolls blind
As a boulder in the night-sea surf,
   And her family troops behind.

The sea-smell enters with them
   As they sidle and slither and spill
With their huge eyes and their tiny eyes
   And a dripping ocean-chill.

Some of her cousins are lobsters
   Some floppy jelly fish –
What would you be if your family tree
   Grew out of such a dish?

Her brothers are crabs jointed and knobbed
   With little pinhead eyes,
Their pincers crack the biscuits
   And they bubble joyful cries.

Crayfish the size of ponies
   Creak as they sip their milk.
My father stares in horror
   At my mother's secret ilk.

They wave long whiplash antennae,
  They sizzle and they squirt –
We smile and waggle our fingers back
  Or grandma would be hurt.

'What's new, Ma?' my father asks,
  'Down in the marvellous deep?'
Her face swells up, her eyes bulge huge
  And she begins to weep.

She knots her sucker tentacles
  And gapes like a nestling bird,
And her eyes flash, changing stations,
  As she attempts a WORD –

Then out of her eyes there brim two drops
  That plop into her saucer –
And that is all she manages,
  And my Dad knows he can't force her.

And when they've gone, my ocean-folk,
  No man could prove they came –
For the sea-tears in her saucer
  And a man's tears are the same.

My Brother Bert

Pets are the Hobby of my brother Bert.
He used to go to school with a Mouse in his shirt.

His Hobby it grew, as some hobbies will,
And grew and GREW and GREW until –

Oh don't breathe a word, pretend you haven't heard.
A simply appalling thing has occurred –

The very thought makes me iller and iller:
Bert's brought home a gigantic Gorilla!

If you think that's really not such a scare,
What if it quarrels with his Grizzly Bear?

You still think you could keep your head?
What if the Lion from under the bed

And the four Ostriches that deposit
Their football eggs in his bedroom closet

And the Aardvark out of his bottom drawer
All danced out and joined in the Roar?

What if the Pangolins were to caper
Out of their nests behind the wallpaper?

With the fifty sorts of Bats
That hang on his hatstand like old hats,

And out of a shoebox the excitable Platypus
Along with the Ocelot or Jungle-Cattypus?

The Wombat, the Dingo, the Gecko, the Grampus –
How they would shake the house with their Rumpus!

Not to forget the Bandicoot
Who would certainly peer from his battered old boot.

Why it could be a dreadful day,
And what Oh what would the neighbours say!

My Aunt

You've heard how a green thumb
Makes flowers come
Quite without toil
Out of any old soil.

Well, my Aunt's thumbs were green.
At a touch, she had blooms
Of prize Chrysanthemums –
The grandest ever seen.

People from miles around
Came to see those flowers
And were truly astounded
By her unusual powers.

One day a little weed
Pushed up to drink and feed
Among the pampered flowers
At her water-can showers.

Day by day it grew
With ragged leaves and bristles
Till it was tall as me or you –
It was a King of Thistles.

'Prizes for flowers are easy,'
My Aunt said in her pride.
'But was there ever such a weed
The whole world wide?'

She watered it, she tended it,
It grew alarmingly.
As if I had offended it,
It bristled over me.

'Oh Aunt!' I cried. 'Beware of that!
I saw it eat a bird.'
She went on polishing its points
As if she hadn't heard.

'Oh Aunt!' I cried. 'It has a flower
Like a lion's beard –'
Too late! It was devouring her
Just as I had feared!

Her feet were waving in the air –
But I shall not proceed.
Here ends the story of my Aunt
And her ungrateful weed.

40

My Aunt Flo

Horrible! Horrible! Horrible is my old Aunt Flo!
Yet very, very ordinary, I would have you know.
A tidy garden of roses, and a tiny tidy house.
She does not need a cat because there's nothing for a
mouse.

Nevertheless horribly nightly
She goes straight up the chimney lightly
Or through the wall, and not on a broom
But astride a huge mushroom,
A poisonous, red, white-spotted killer
Grown on corpses in her cellar –

She goes straight up about one hundred yards
Then flattens out and aims for Scotland
Or maybe Germany and as she goes
She rips her false face off and reveals her true one
Like a gigantic grasshopper.

My Aunt Flo's kindly smile is round and happy as an
apple.
A bit of a girl in her day but now as proper as a chapel.
On Sunday in the choir her fine soprano can't be missed
Or at the Women's Institute the accomplished pianist.

Nevertheless nightly her laughter
Burrows in graveyards where she's after
Dead bodies which she will boil
And render down for witch's oil –
Oil which she keeps in old gin bottles
For her supernatural battles.

A new-buried baby she will go three hundred miles
   for, it is a fact.
Its fingerbones for this, its toebones for that –
   horrible!
And men's dried features and women's vital parts
   hang in her attic
Dusty as dry herbs.

Her Sunday teas are cosy, with her cups so delicate.
A single crust-less sandwich of cucumber on your plate,
The crumb upon her smiling lip recovered daintily,
And after that a biscuit and another cup of tea.

But you never saw her where
She leaps at the moon in the shape of a hare,
Or bobs ahead of you or follows
In a weasel's shape, or wallows
Under the pleasure-cruiser's bows
In dolphin-shape, or reaches to browse

Your hair at midnight in the likeness of a donkey.
Did she pass your window, was that her?
A giant sow is already asleep in your bed, ten to one.
You saw her in the distance? Just a glance? For certain
You will wake up tonight with a frog in your mouth.

44

My Uncle Dan

My Uncle Dan's an inventor, you may think that's very
 fine.
You may wish he was your Uncle instead of being
 mine –
If he wanted he could make a watch that bounces when
 it drops,
He could make a helicopter out of string and bottle tops
Or any really useful thing you can't get in the shops.
  But Uncle Dan has other ideas:
  The bottomless glass for ginger beers,
  The toothless saw that's safe for the tree,
  A special word for a spelling bee
  (Like Lionocerangoutangadder),
  Or the roll-uppable rubber ladder,
  The mystery pie that bites when it's bit –
  My Uncle Dan invented it.
My Uncle Dan sits in his den inventing night and day.
His eyes peer from his hair and beard like mice from a
 load of hay.
And does he make the shoes that will go walks without
 your feet?
A shrinker to shrink instantly the elephants you meet?
A carver that just carves from the air steaks cooked and
 ready to eat?

No, no, he has other intentions –
Only perfectly useless inventions:
Glassless windows (they never break),
A medicine to cure the earthquake,
The unspillable screwed-down cup,
The stairs that go neither down nor up,
The door you simply paint on a wall –
Uncle Dan invented them all.

My Uncle Mick

My Uncle Mick the portrait artist painted Nature's
    Creatures.
Began with the Venus Fly-trap but he soon got on to
    Leeches
Because he found inspiring beauty in their hideous
    features.

His portrait of the Lamprey, whose face is a living
    grave,
Knocked men cold with horror, made women quake
    and rave.
'When you have seen what's what,' he said, 'That's
    how you *should* behave.'

He painted a lifesize portrait of a laughing Alligator
With a man's feet sticking out, and titled 'THE CREATOR
DOING REPAIRS AND MAINTENANCE INSIDE HIS
EXCAVATOR'.

'The bigger the fright,' said Uncle Mick, 'The more it
    can inspire us.'
He filled his ceiling with the portrait of a vicious virus.
Out of his walls came sharks with jaws like doorways to
    devour us.

But alas his fate was waiting when he painted a tiger's
 roar.
We found his paints and brushes scattered round upon
 the floor.
Had the tiger got him? Uncle Mick was seen no more.

We gaze at the Tiger's portrait now. Was that my
 Uncle's fate?
His painting was too lifelike and his rescuers were too
 late.
Those eyes glare dumbly back at us and our hair stands
 up straight.

My Mother

All mothers can serve up a bit of buttered toast,
Most mothers can handle a pie or a roast,
A few can boil a shark à la Barbary Coast,
But when I say mine can COOK – it's no boast.

When the Maharajah of old Srinigar
Wishes to make himself popular
Who can help him out but my Ma?
With elephant loads of nuts and suet,
With hundreds of coolies to trample through it
(To stir it you see), she produces a Cake
As huge as a palace that architects make –
Frosted and crusted with pink and blue icing.
Oh think of the knife they need for the slicing!

But special dishes are more to her wishes –
Nutritious, delicious, peculiar dishes –
Not just kippers in carrot juice,
But Buffalo Puff and Whipped-Cream Goose,
A Bouillabaisse out of no cook-book pages
With Whale and Walrus in collops and wedges
And festoons of Octopus over the edges.
(And should that give you the slightest uneasiness
There's Rose Crush topped with a peach's fleeciness.)

Sautéd Ant Eggs on Champagne Alligator
Are wonderful with a baked potato!
I took her a rattlesnake that had attacked us:
She served it up curried with Crème de la Cactus.

Her kitchen is a continual crisis,
Billowing clouds of aromas and spices –
Bubbling cauldrons and humming ovens,
Pans spitting by sixes, pots steaming by sevens.

Most mothers stick to their little cook-books,
But this is the way *my* Mother cooks!

My Father

Some fathers work at the office, others work at the
    store,
Some operate great cranes and build up skyscrapers
    galore,
Some work in canning factories counting green peas
    into cans,
Some drive all night in huge and thundering removal
    vans.

But mine has the strangest job of the lot.
My Father's the Chief Inspector of – What?
O don't tell the mice, don't tell the moles,
My Father's the Chief Inspector of HOLES.

It's a work of the highest importance because you never
    know
What's in a hole, what fearful thing is creeping from
    below.
Perhaps it's a hole to the ocean and will soon gush
    water in tons,
Or maybe it leads to a vast cave full of gold and
    skeletons.

Though a hole might seem to have nothing but dirt
    in,
Somebody's simply got to make certain.
Caves in the mountain, clefts in the wall,
My father has to inspect them all.

That crack in the road looks harmless. My Father knows it's not.
The world may be breaking into two and starting at that spot.
Or maybe the world is a great egg, and we live on the shell,
And it's just beginning to split and hatch: you simply cannot tell.

> If you see a crack, run to the phone, run!
> My Father will know just what's to be done.
> A rumbling hole, a silent hole,
> My Father will soon have it under control.

Keeping a check on all these holes he hurries from morning to night.
There might be sounds of marching in one, or an eye shining bright.
A tentacle came groping from a hole that belonged to a mouse,
A floor collapsed and Chinamen swarmed up into the house.

> A Hole's an unpredictable thing –
> Nobody knows what a Hole might bring.
> Caves in the mountain, clefts in the wall,
> My Father has to inspect them all!

My Own True Family

Once I crept in an oakwood – I was looking for a stag.
I met an old woman there – all knobbly stick and rag.
She said: 'I have your secret here inside my little bag.'

Then she began to cackle and I began to quake.
She opened up her little bag and I came twice awake –
Surrounded by a staring tribe and me tied to a stake.

They said: 'We are the oak-trees and your own true
family.
We are chopped down, we are torn up, you do not blink
an eye.
Unless you make a promise now – now you are going to
die.

Whenever you see an oak-tree felled, swear now you
will plant two.
Unless you swear the black oak bark will wrinkle over
you
And root you among the oaks where you were born but
never grew.'

This was my dream beneath the boughs, the dream that
altered me.
When I came out of the oakwood, back to human
company,
My walk was the walk of a human child, but my heart
was a tree.